IN A STONE'S HOLLOW

IN A STONE'S HOLLOW

Poems by

Freddy Frankel

First Edition 2 3 4 5 6 7 8 9

Library of Congress Cataloging in Publication Data
Freddy Frankel,
In a Stone's Hollow
ISBN 13: 978-0-9771973-6-1
ISBN 10: 0-9771973-6-0
Library of Congress Control Number: 2007921812

Fairweather Books is an imprint of
Bedbug Press, Inc.
P.O. Box 39
Brownsville, OR 97327
www.bedbugpress.com

Author photo and artifact photos: Guy Hofstein
Cover photo of Soweto Uprising: © Sam Nzima
Design: Cheryl McLean

Printed by Lynx Group, Salem, Oregon.

This book is printed on acid-free paper.

for my wife, Betty,
and our grandchildren, all of them

Acknowledgments

Several poems—some under different titles, some in earlier versions—have appeared or are forthcoming in the following publications to whose editors the author is grateful:

Ibbetson Street: "10 January 1945," "20 January 1945," "Smoking," "Black Jew / White Jew," "Schadenfreude"
Lasell Village Voice: "At the Hector Pieterson Memorial"
Moment: "Cycling"
Passager: "Maze"
Pudding House Publications: Chapbook, "Hottentot Venus: Poems of Apartheid"
Rough Places Plain, Anthology: "15 March 1945," "3 April 1945"
The Anthology of New England Writers, 2004: "3 April 1945"
The Iconoclast: "Cape Town–Johannesburg Boat-Train"
The Mercy of Tides, Anthology: "Surfing"
The Larcom Review: "Garden-boy," "The Letter," "The Pass Law," "Transvaal, 1950"

I also wish to acknowledge:

Susan and the late Frank Anthony of New England Writers for finding me in 2003;

Tony Gorsline of Bedbug Press and Vern Rutsala, distinguished poet, for affirming me in 2005;

my niece Annette Emdon of Johannesburg, an authority on copyright, for leading me to Sam Nzima, photojournalist, and his agent, Heidi Smith, who have been most gracious in allowing me to use the picture of the Soweto Uprising;

my friend Guy Hofstein, retired professional photographer, for his interest and invaluable help in creating the photographs of the military artifacts;

Kristin McKean, family friend, for the photo of Ariana, my new grandchild from China;

Katie Warrener, for her careful and painstaking proofreading;

Cheryl McLean, for her constant good humor and attention to detail in designing this book;

Diana Der-Hovanessian, Robert Brustein, and Vern Rutsala, for their kind words of encouragement;

and last but not least, Barbara Helfgott Hyett and her Workshop for Publishing Poets, for teaching me and guiding me over the past eight years.

Contents

Part Two: Hottentot Venus: Poems of Apartheid

Part Three: Bound Close on the Naked Vine

Part One

Notes on a War, '44–'46

Preface

I was twenty and halfway through my medical training when
I enlisted as a corporal in the South African army. During the
eighteen months on active service in the north of Italy, I kept a log
in a small brown leather notebook that I carried in my knapsack.
In it I briefly jotted down events from my personal experience and
that of others. When I came home I put the notebook in a metal
box with my service medals, ribbons, name tags, and a charm in a
linen pouch I wore around my neck. I didn't visit there in almost
sixty years.

The poems reflect the collaboration of the self I am with the self I
was and, in a few, the memories of others grafted on to mine.

My dream is to will down the firmament,
place in every human soul a star
where vengeance lurks.

Notebook
(*author*)
March 1945

12 June 1944

Johannesburg, South Africa

I hop off the tram at the Drill Hall
into the skirl of bagpipes, elated
by the thrill—I'm underage,
my mother begged me not to volunteer.

On the other side of the wrought iron fence
men drill on hard red clay;
khaki shirts and kilts of plaid
yield to the sergeant's shrill command

and wheel like a tightly woven cloth;
their ribbon bars—stripes of orange,
gold, and blue—medals earned
in the African campaign.

A woman glares—my tweed coat, white shirt,
and knitted tie conspicuous. Ill at ease
I go to the recruitment hut,
wait in line, look straight ahead.

I sign my name, lie that I am twenty-one.
It will be the death of me
my mother said—the pipes wail
War's a killing place!

16 June 1944

Johannesburg

The game subsides with taps
on this first night in the barracks—
the horny jokes about the pinup girls,
the ribald laughter. I hunker

in my bunk, my kit bag on the shelf above;
new fatigues, khaki shirts and pants, thick long johns;
leather boots, sturdy silver grommets
for the thongs; a khaki beret called a *cunt cap*,

its creases tightly folded like my gut. Two name tags
on a chain around my neck stamped *545038v*
Jewish. In the dark the rustle of a rosary,
heavy breathing, a stifled gasp.

15 August 1944

Aden, Yemen

We sail from Durban, the land strip fades.
Two weeks later brown hills rise up from a sea
spread smooth like molten wax beneath the sun.
I hail a cab—a bearded man in caftan,

stains and tattered sleeves—ask him for the synagogue,
ride through dusty streets and archways past pedestrians
in sandals, men in turbans, camels; a kiosk
selling spices, the air is thick with cardamom and cloves.

The driver stops and points, a shabby building peeling paint.
I pat my pocket, touch the swollen envelope
my mother gave me—in her hand:
For the first poor Jew you meet across the sea.

2 September 1944

HMS Ormonde

Midway from Egypt to Italy we're on deck:
Australians returning to war; South Africans—
recruits like me and the Cape Corps knee-deep
in their colored isolation; and

young Jews from Palestine. We speak softly
over deep blue water shot with snow.
Abraham Margovsky, Third Battalion,
Palestine, shakes my hand.

His parents wove the water
through dry land; now
willows hang low in the wadis, oranges rotate
their navels to the sun,

a hundred thousand flowers trace
the contours of the desert sand.
Abraham tells me, *It is good*—
like the God in Genesis.

4 September 1944

HMS *Ormonde*

In the blackout
I muddle through the curtain maze
that leads into the lounge
for Other Ranks.

Tobacco smoke in layers fills the air;
there are no chairs, men sit on their haunches
and talk of exploits, sip the canteen's watery tea.
I'm preoccupied with war,

the soldier in me. I can fix a splint, inject morphine, but
should I know
where booby traps are set; one fellow warns me,
The laden branches on a cherry tree;

another, *The hearth in an abandoned farmhouse.*
Will I remember
where the road bends—
or recognize the North Star!

7 October 1944

Taranto, Italy

Here in the slums of the city's night
buildings are buried,
the cicatrix of a naked chimney stoops,
our billet is a shanty with a lean-to.

Our beds, boards on concrete
blocks; our fireplace, a metal drum with holes,
rusted; we are not heroes,
just in rehearsal for a play about war.

A crystal voice
like that belonging to a choirboy
sings O *Sole Mio*
out there somewhere in the dark.

10 November 1944

Bari

A tattered banner flails
from the canopy of the Opera House,
Rigoletto leaks through
broken windows. Outside the church—

its chancel wounded by a bomb—
boys push and shove, kick a tin can.
A scrawny pigeon splatters on the cobblestones.
Germans stomped these streets in packs,

painted swastikas on the walls,
now Fascisti burrow underground.
My father was a German Jew who left the Rhineland
in his teens. I march with Allied troops in boots, here,

where old men are weighed down,
and women hold the edges of their coats
closed against the chill—and children play
without a ball.

10 January 1945

Arezzo

Today's my mother's birthday,
she didn't want me
in this war, wouldn't sign
the army forms....

Men *always think they know*
she said, *the ugly truth*
comes in the personal effects
sent home.

In this dark farmhouse
there is cold ash in the grate,
and the orchard is settled
under snow

deserted
but for blackbirds
waiting
for something to happen.

20 January 1945

Arezzo

I rehearse how to act when there,
play cool, as if this isn't new.
Her husband, a retired teacher, is at home,
I impress him with the size

of my vocabulary, forget that my Italian thrives
on raw infinitives:
I to go; I to eat; I to want. It started
when her brown eyes darted

down my army uniform—
she handed me my laundry, invited me
to supper at her home. She washes shirts
and underwear for soap and margarine.

We sit around the table,
her husband checks my verbs,
she leans to illustrate a point,
a prow of breast spills over. Lost in the fold

I confuse the present with the future tense.
She sees me to the door, gives me a kiss,
draws my hand inside her blouse,
You must to learn to touch, she says.

25 January 1945

Arezzo

Indians are segregated in South Africa,
I've never been this close to a Sikh before—
a well-made man, handsome beard
and a smell of foreign spice,

his khaki turban stained with blood.
He speaks about it calmly,
a nonevent: three men in town threw rocks
because he's Sikh.

Let me see the wound, I say. He sits,
uncoils his turban, right hand circles
round his head, tosses yards of muslin to his left.
Blood oozes slowly from the scalp,

glossy black hair drops below his shoulders.
I pick up scissors; he, *Don't cut!*
I do, shave around the wound
then stitch—

a gash not quite an inch.
Half bowed he sighs,
says nothing.
Disinfectant would have been enough....

10 February 1945

Castelnuovo

She thumbs a ride, climbs in
the back with four of us
and takes the bench across from me.
It's almost dusk, she's pretty,

oval eyes, long eyelashes.
Her shoes have wooden soles, worn straps.
Knitted stockings reach her knees,
her woolen skirt, the crescent of her thighs.

The truck swerves off the road that takes you
to the village with no name, then stops.
She remains, we get out. Then leg over tailgate
the driver vanishes under the canvas top.

I can't see in the dark but hear them.
He checks his belt when he climbs out,
the buttons on his fly.
The next man takes his turn—

I wonder if they pay—or she likes men
a lot. In queer excitement,
inexperienced, I want to move away
but disconnected stand and wait.

25 February 1945

Near Castiglione

With screeching intermittency
the shells explode—the village
tumbles in a hideous breach—
vultures strip the earth of rind.

At night I pass a man who scrapes
the fallen masonry to one side
with his crutch, swings his half leg
back and forth, like a pendulum

contradicting time. He finds two metal pots,
a picture frame,
the woman at his side bends down
to pick them up.

I roam the ruins, find my billet, my twisted cot;
fall into the pivot of my senses, sleep
until sleep melts, gives way to dawn—
and its deformities.

28 February 1945

The Apennines

It could have been an easy rout,
we had them covered
in a stand of pine trees
where the hollow rises on the other side.

Reconnaissance reported five.
The officer, blond and tall,
lovely in his uniform, came down
the slope; the paper in his hand a map.

He whistled softly, unafraid,
reached the arc below the wall,
dropped his trousers, crouched,
a bloom of naked sunlight on his German thigh

beyond the jurisdiction of his generals.
From our roving household in the woods
we looked on in silence,
no one fired a shot.

1 March 1945

The Apennines

At dusk I move away from men at war
to a stone's hollow on a hill, my perch
where the wind sweeps forgotten leaves
through winter in the woodlot.

I lean to the tug of earth, that cold tilt,
and long—long to smooth my palms
over the contours of your cheeks,
the alcoves of your ears, your hair;

have you meet my skin eyes closed,
have you lift my hands and bring them
to your lips, these wooden and unpracticed
fingertips.

9 March 1945

The Apennines

Found at dawn—impaled
on barbed wire
spirals wound around
the prison block—

a gray green
German uniform.
Eyes too deep to shed a tear—
his body dances slow

in useless arabesques
to disengage—
before
the sniper's enfilade.

15 March 1945

The Apennines

Should God have quit Creation on day five,
those birds, those waters spellbound in the bay!
Men hunting men in mountains to survive

we ask for mercy as we run, shrivel
under cover while bullets ricochet.
Should God have quit Creation on day five—

day six He made a man, so sure he'd thrive;
now look, we bag torn body parts each day,
men hunting men in mountains to survive!

Some luckless soldiers won't get out alive,
still young they'll change back to dirt and clay.
Should God have quit Creation on day five.

In the widespread killing, the snowfall driven,
peace drags, sinking on its unploughed way—
men hunting men in mountains to survive

under this hell's dome. I've panicked and I've
embraced Him, cursed Him for this blood-iron fray.
Should God have quit Creation on day five,
men hunting men in mountains to survive.

3 April 1945

Assisi

A bomb twisted the windows from their sockets,
shrunk rooms to rubble, doors swung
from the heartless walls.
Blood-soaked trousers clinging to my thighs

I sat, a stunned silhouette in the buckled jeep.
Christ stood outside the church, bronze,
as tall as a soldier,
neither his rod nor his staff could comfort me.

From my hospital bed
I look out on pastures spared by war,
olive groves, vineyards, leafy tongues of early spring,
starlings—St. Francis used to feed them from his hand.

My bandaged thigh unhinged between white sheets,
I think of how my grandpa makes a blessing,
winds the leather tefillin down his arm,
his breath anoints each word. I want so much to pray.

20 April 1945

Montemario

The sergeant hands out mail,
I recognize my father's script
and take it to my bunk to read.
He's fifty-three today, he lost his job,

he says it's not bad, he'll be okay.
I pull his picture from my wallet,
smooth lips stretched into a smile that sets
like clay. Try to sort my love for him—

like the knotted maple
in the cabinet he made with beveled glass—
the dovetail joints so tight
they could have grown that way.

I watched him hit those nailheads only once
to flatten them, metal mottled on the wood.
He taught me: *Hold the hammer straight—*
hit hard, boy—the only way!

25 April 1945

Rome

We're partly nude or bare-assed
in the washroom when we shave,
the latrines have eleven seats,
there are twelve heads in the shower room.

When reporting sick they have us strip
to the soles of our feet. No one seems to mind—
but there's routine *short arm inspection,*
the army hunt for venereal disease:

we move in a line close to a hundred
past the doctor who sits
on the edge of his stool;
one by one we loosen belts, unbutton flies,

drop our underpants down our thighs;
his eyes peer into every crotch,
he tells us—everyone—
pull the foreskin back.

8 May 1945

Rome

For fourteen days men say
and unsay this and that.
Il Duce's been hanged by his heels.
Peals from the campanile end the war.

Before the delirium cools
it petrifies the petals
of blood, the souls dispersed
like pollen—

too many for God to count
the millions one by one—
and no one yet speaks the word
Hiroshima, that distant city.

6 June 1945

Milan

The man who comes to sit at my table
wears a gold signet ring,
he holds a cabbage leaf, dried and rolled,
in the O of his thumb and forefinger—

smokes it as if it were a good cigar.
I light up an army-issue *Players*—
he stares at me, the ribbons
on my chest, then at the pack.

A *thousand lire*, I signal with one finger
knowing it's illegal; he slides notes
across the table underneath his hand, the Fascist icon—
rods and a projecting blade—carved into the ring.

I hesitate a nanosecond taken by surprise,
The man has balls, I think—
his mouth in a twisted smile,
his eyes cold as cobalt.

21 June 1945

On a letter from home

My cousin Ruth was pressed against the doorjamb—
her right cheek bruised and swollen—punched by the SS
to loosen her grip on her father's arm.
They dragged him away.

She was my age, attractive blue eyes and black hair
I was told. That night they returned to rape her.
In a prison camp a hundred miles away
Jews climbed down from cattle trucks,

the shaved voice of the officer rose
from the platform. He sorted men like a forester thins trees,
the sturdy lined up on the left—the rest, including Uncle Felix,
hero of the First World War, to the right,

the road to the mills of darkness. Uncle, after you left
did you think they'd return to rape her,
that your daughter would take her life,
gas from the kitchen stove? God must have seen it all.

10 September 1945

Lake Maggiore

Under storm's wing weighed down with cloud
the lake can be as heavy as hammered lead.
Tonight it's unblemished,

war is done, I'm waiting to begin
my journey home. Below
illegible stars

swallows glide on the watersmooth,
and men and women dance underneath this arbor
on the bank.

I watch Lina Lazaroni in her chiffon dress,
the pendant I gave her nestles
in the cleavage that defies her clothes.

3 February 1946

Johannesburg

My Aunty Bella fled the Rhineland,
came to live with us, I was thirteen.
When I went to war
she sewed this stone inside a linen pouch

with a leather strap,
for me to wear around my neck
till I come home.
I've not looked at it till now,

this small stone, square, flat
and metal gray, not more
than half an inch across.
It was plucked from gravel

on Rabbi Eliezer's grave.
May he rest, she said. *It's for mazel,*
he was a holy man,
he brought miracles.

PART TWO

Hottentot Venus: Poems of Apartheid

Preface

The racist culture in South Africa was deeply rooted in the fabric of daily life from the time of the earliest white settlers. As an adult living there, I was never entirely free of the guilt and embarrassment associated with my privileged life. After the political victory of the Afrikaners in 1948, interracial tensions were aggravated by the increasingly white supremacist ideology of the government and the growing rage of millions of subjugated black people. While writing these poems in recent years, I relived the helplessness of being virtually disenfranchised in the 1950s as a member of a small Jewish minority. I made the decision to emigrate after the massacre at Sharpeville in 1960, not without sadness, nor a sense of disloyalty to those I left behind. Few could have prophesied the bloodless transfer of power in the 1990s to the majority of the people under Nelson Mandela.

When I Am Six

Benoni, 1930

Servants shake our sheets,
make beds, down on their knees
polish our floors. Their rooms,
a shabby building near the fence;
their chairs, wooden boxes;
beds, mattress ticking wrapped
round coconut husk.
Maud sometimes lets me in
her door to sniff the stiff
pomade that straightens hair.
When her boyfriend William steps
out of our outhouse, Aunt Alice
hurrying to get in is shocked.
My father builds a shed
in a far corner of the yard,
says servants squat
on beams between two posts,
don't need a toilet seat
above the pail.

Kapenzi, Our Cook

I love the way she slices bread,
pats sandwiches I take to school.
This evening I see her to the bus—
the smell of diesel fumes,
the shudder of the engine while it idles
as the servants scramble on.
They laugh, talk, too many
for the ride, some will have to wait.
Kapenzi gets a seat and waves
through the window
as she swings away. Walking
here she took my hand inside
her palm, I drew it back,
fiddled with the laces
as if I had to tie my shoe.

The House-boy Bathes

Naked in his room
in the back of the yard,
his brown torso glows
through the lather above his crotch.
He empties a pail of water
on his head—figure in a fountain,
polished marble column
in the rain—belly taut
as a leather strop
from ribs to pelvic rim,
further down well-sprung
thighs, calves, feet.
Alone in my house
I stand at the bathroom mirror,
limbs lank, groin bare as truth.
Fetch my brother's jockstrap,
watch a ten-year-old
bulge his biceps posing
in the empty pouch.

Benoni Is a White Town

Hitler floats down Africa
on the radio,
to a grid of straight streets,
square houses—my hometown
gray as the dirty white sand
of the mine dump that looms
at the bottom of the road.
Cocopans like ants in single file
crawl up the slope, tip their contents
and roll down the other side.
On a bench behind my hedge
I struggle to remember Russian
names in *War and Peace*.
Kids dribble a ball in the street,
Van Rensburg boasts
he scored a goal, Shapiro shouts,
A *foul!* Van Rensburg yells,
You bloody Jew!

Note: *Ben-oni* is a biblical name
meaning "Son of my sorrow"

The Mine-boy's Final Visit
to My Uncle's Kaffir Store

He breathes the concentrate of smells:
open bins of sugar, packets
of ground coffee, kerosene dripping
from its drum onto the wooden floor;
leather boots hanging by their laces,
flannel shirts piled high.
His labor contract at an end he's headed home—
Basutoland—in a serge khaki poncho
and a cone hat of straw.

He fingers a Jew's harp, an alarm clock,
taps the coins in his open palm, counts
them. Points to a dozen blankets
hanging from a beam, asks me
to unhook the checkered pink one
for the wife he hasn't seen in years.
He grabs a fist of candy pellets
given free to all the customers,
hurries with his package to the door.

Cycling

Six Afrikaans boys head me off
from behind the church—
their leader van Niekerk in untied boots,
his father in jail.
He thrusts his stubbled chin, spits words,
New bike, man!

Three grab the saddle, two the handlebar,
hoist me off the ground, a prisoner in air.
Van Niekerk opens pages in my prayer book,
You riding to the Jew-boy school,
what's that stupid wiggle there...?
An aleph, I say.

A what? he asks, runs his snot across the words,
tears out leaves, gives them to the wind.
They jeer, then set me free—silent
as they watch me
get off my bike, pick up prayers,
touch each to my lips.

Lesson of the Day at Hebrew School

Mrs. Shtayn from Poland
begins her class. The tea-boy enters,
a Zulu man with trousers ending
at the knee,
places the tray beside her books.
His feet are bare, she stares
until he's out the door;
puts a cube of sugar on her tongue,
puckers her mouth in a kiss.

With cup in hand she sucks tea
through her lips,
we hope she'll dribble on her chin.
When I get home I ask the cook for tea
with sugar cubes, grip one in my teeth.
My mother strains to be English,
protests with genteel vowels,
Son, that's coarse—
just like a foreign Jew!

My Mother's Jewish Accent

In the presence of the English
my mother widened her mouth,
exhaled the new angular words
unfolding on her unathletic tongue.

The tutor came, I watched from the garden
as she read, separating syllables into a string of pearls;
lips rounded to free the diphthongs *house—spouse*;
droning *this—that*, the dentals forced against her teeth.

Then I saw her stand before the mirror, inflating
her cheeks and her chest, in small bursts hammering
Out, damned spot! Out, I say! My mother, my favorite
person, lost to me—becoming somebody else.

The Letter

Dear Mother, I am fine....
                              Ludwig

My eyes are at the level of the counter
my father grips with trembling hands.
Leaning forward, his eyebrows touch the rail,
he pleads in Afrikaans,
Please give me my letter,
I shouldn't have put it in the mail....
The clerk leads us to an inner office,

the postmaster doesn't even nod his head;
at the sorting table labeled *Mail*
for Overseas he spreads the pile—
at least a hundred letters. My father finds his
envelope, white linen finish, German script;
he reads the second line,
We think Hitler is a schweinehund....

I know that means *pig-dog.*
The postmaster tears the page,
flings bits into the basket on the floor,
fills in a report.
In baggy pants my father doesn't move,
keeps repeating, *Sorry I'm causing all this fuss.*
I wish I wasn't here.

Cape Town–Johannesburg Boat-train

The engine's polished belly bowls along the platform's length,
flings elbows, whistles, screeches. Halts.
Down the years, dispossessed, my German family
steps off the Wednesday morning train.
Uncle Heinrich,

thrown out of his faculty—the only Jew—
the first to come in long black coat with one valise.
Ludwig, who'd been a lawyer, peddles bras and petticoats,
Fritz and Liesel grow another shop with kitsch,
Max, the doctor, trundles stretchers through halls.

At gatherings in our living room their laughter comes
in boisterous foreign phonemes, cigar smoke hangs midair,
and Gunther standing close strokes women's hips.
Uncle Gustav preens as if he'd owned a castle on the Rhine.
Sometimes they tell of how it was before they got away.

Black Jew / White Jew

Eight men and my Lithuanian grandpa
wrapped in his prayer shawl, wait
for a tenth man at the heavy wooden door. Outside
on the steps of Park Street *shul*, sheen
on the sleeves and seat of his navy blue suit,
a black man tells them
he's a Jew, wants to come in to pray.

Grandpa firmly shakes his head—
he signals to me with his finger, I come in.
From the back bench of the sanctuary
I see him bend his body forward,
bob back, add momentum to his prayers.
I try to understand the nature of his piety,
wind the leather strap of my tefillin
down my arm, bind my torn belief.

Gross Anatomy

Witwatersrand Medical School

Kumalo, the one black student in the class,
and I stand among the dead lying face up
on marble slabs. We're assigned
to work at table twenty-one.

Our body is a Zulu male, grotesque
holes in his earlobes—colored discs
removed before a technician pickled him.
I look at a white woman on a distant slab

relieved she's not on ours. Unlikely a black
man would ever have seen her naked when alive.
Kumalo sits at our cadaver, holds the scalpel steady,
cuts a straight line penetrating just the skin

from elbow to thumbnail; deftly
separates arteries from veins, lifts hair-thin nerves,
displays sheaves of muscle, the housing
layer by layer.

Pleurisy

In a crowded non-European ward

Beneath a bed occupied by a patient in coma
lies a fevered man on a mattress on the floor.
Nine students stand in line ahead of me
to listen to his chest. In turn, resting on both knees,
we crouch low, inch under the bed
to get to his ribs. His warm soaked nightshirt

pushed aside reveals glistening skin;
I set the bell end of my stethoscope
on the blue ring mapped there by the intern
and say, *Keep breathing deep.*
The gritty membranes grate against each other—
like leather scraping leather.

Zululand

Scattered cattle graze
on the tides of green grass,
Zulus punctuate the slopes
to and from their beehive huts.

A woman, bare breasts,
beaded collar resting on her throat,
plods her way, her head
a steady pedestal for a pail of water.

From another hill a man shouts,
Saakoo bawna,
she returns his greeting,
Yebbo, beckons him,

Eezaapa!
The long vowels propel the wind,
elongate the echo,
he makes his way across.

Surfing

Cape St. Francis, South Africa

Let me wade out to meet it
where the water rises two miles wide
from its shelf,
mount it, stand
and grip my board
with naked soles—

the wave rolls in, won't melt,
won't quit, split, or section.
I squat beneath the curl—ride,
ride across the face of the waterwall
like a kindred current.

Game Reserve

From her haunches
the hindmost doe bleeds.
Wild Cape hunting dogs have ripped
her in the chase. She crumples,
rises, sinks into the high triandra grass.

One dog clamps her neck in its fangs....

In that heat and hymn of cicadas,
destiny's indifference, dogs lap
meat from the bone without greed—
without pride.

Garden-boy

Weekends we lean upon the handle of the pick,
together lever rocks, heave gray slate
slabs to pave my garden walks,
prune deadwood, sculpt hedges.
He wheels loam across my lawn for me
to rake. We sometimes touch—

our fingers on the handle, or the hosepipe.
When he's sick I listen with my stethoscope,
his skin brown over ribs
like membrane on a drum,
my fingertips against the muscles of his belly—
but I never shake his hand.

Regardless of the ban I sometimes hold out
beer for Makson Maluleka. He closes the bottle
in his palm like a part of his fist,
ambles from my stoop toward the yard
walled in by servants' rooms.
There he drinks, behind my house, alone.

Cook-girl

Constant as her starched white pinafore,
she comes into my kitchen
from across the yard
each dawn.
Carries fermented porridge
out each noon to spoon
onto the servants' plates;
sets the table
in my dining room each night,

she's been with me for years.
One morning she's not here,
no note, no word.
She reappears
on the other side of town
in a new uniform.
I had just installed a shower
and a lightbulb
in her room.

The Pass Law

Every Sunday
the garden-boy in my last year's suit
at the kitchen door,
sends cook to ask me for his pass.

Maluleka's ready to go out!
I bring the slip of paper to the kitchen,
Please pass bearer Maluleka
to Alexandra township, to return
by six tonight.

I warn him to be careful—the police—
the shebeen. He hides behind his smile,
I'm good, my master.
Thanks, my master, for the pass.

Grief and Grievance

After the funeral
of my neighbor's infant son,
roses and delphiniums
on the tables, orchids
on the mantel, people stand
in clusters. In the kitchen
the house-boy washes teacups,
eyes fixed on the sink.
A year ago he lost
his daughter, picked wild
baby's breath to decorate
her grave. Grief and grievance
softly rise and fall,
servants carry trays, *Tea for madam,*
would the master like some tea?

Transvaal, 1950

If heaven wanted us to mix,
heaven would have made us all the same.
Senior minister,
Dutch Reformed Church

Among his cooking pots, spirit stove,
splintered bed and splintered table,
cartons, clothes and cloths,
and a battered leather suitcase
bearing my initials,
Maluleka squats. He's the father
of my garden-boy,
I gave it to him when the handle broke.
The elders of the tribe remained
when children left,
live in mud-and-grass-roofed huts,
turn the earth with an ox-drawn plough.
Pangeni—fertile valley snatched
by edict from this Bantu clan—
will now be white.
The government will move them
in army trucks, on unmade roads
to some place distant on the veld.

Resignation

I wandered at a distance
from the concrete pipes stacked
like cells in honeycombs,
beyond the cardboard
shacks and corrugated iron
that sprout like wild grass
crowding shantytown;
the children who drift
in human twilight
close in on their victims
like the sea anemone—
and dust patrols the streets.

I watched the Zulu father in the morgue
identify the body of his son pulled
from a chest of drawers, saw him
kiss the old and indurated scar
disfiguring one shoulder,
and touch with tenderness
the garnished earlobes stretched
by bloodied blue and yellow discs.
I heard the widow cry and saw her
breathing deep and hungry....

Sharpeville

March 21, 1960

Basutos, Tswanas, Zulus wade
narrow township streets
to the wire fence
around the Police Station,
to demonstrate against the Pass.

A woman listens to the speaker,
her baby rides her back inside the trough,
the blanket that comes round
and ties beneath her breast.
She bends her body forward,
cups her hands behind her,
hikes him up.

Bullets split the air.

She who used to peddle apples
at my kitchen door turns, runs, is shot.
She hits the ground facedown,
her arm purposeless
against the body of her child.
Resignation dribbles
from the perforations in his back.

The Night after Sharpeville

I host a dinner party.
The house-boy, white suit, red sash,
brings in the silver soup tureen—my friend
Jonathan says what's on our minds:
They'll take revenge;
we'll all be murdered in our beds!

When the guests leave
I bolt the door, see Mothabe
from my kitchen window
sitting on the doorstep in my yard.
He lays his sash across his knees,
angles his palms like a steeple.

I think we would all have done better
had I given him an extra pound
of tea each week;
we circle round each other
like planets, I never visit
in the servants' rooms.

But for the stranglehold of history
I might have pilfered tea leaves
in twisted strips of newsprint,
he might have had the manners
of an upper class. We are both
poured out like water.

Boycott

Bantu in their thousands,
ten abreast in the ten-mile march
from township to city
because of a hike in bus fare.
They overflow the sidewalk,
spill onto the street.
I drive slowly, look for Sesi
who cleans my house, her boyfriend
Pete, he washes windows.

Some in the procession push
bikes, steer the wheels
with both hands on the handlebar
or one on the saddle.
Shirts and pants hang limp,
shoes worn and out of shape.
The marchers turn their pockets
inside out, *Asinamali*—
they have no money!

Barn Swallows *(Hirundo rustica)*

South Africa, 1962

They fly south six thousand miles, flutter
and scrape their arrival beneath our eaves,

in their beaks bring strands of straw
to line the cups of spittled mud that shield their nests.

Veterans of migration
from a threatened climate to reprieve

in the early bite of winter
they take wing.

Apprehension chafes like a stiff starched collar,
we pack and leave.

Taxi Ride in Boston

The driver asks about my accent—I admit
South African. Raw apartheid backs up
in my memory pool, I see it with eyes
numbed by shame—Benoni, my hometown,
walled-in white, the only blacks
were servants or delivery boys on bikes.

Here's this bare-armed man behind the wheel,
stolid as a tribal chief—
when I was ten I stormed from the table, sure
the pepper grounds in my soup were flecks
from the skin on the cook-boy's arm.

I look back in disbelief—the madness
was contagious and went on for years.
The laws required me when grown
to notify the police if
Makson's girlfriend from the township
slept in my backyard. I never did.

The day his daughter died he sat immobile
in my car, like a bas-relief in bronze
as I drove him to the train.
The station agent didn't have a ticket for him
at the *Whites Only* counter—
the platform for *Nonwhites* was out of bounds
to me.

Dear Master

Letter from the laundry girl, Soweto, 1986

Zulus, Shangaans waste each other's blood.
My grandson shakes his fists, lobs rocks,
runs into the bullets of police.
Someone calls my neighbor's son *impimpi*.
I hear it through my window, see
flaming petrol on his shoulders
swallow up his head.
The sky gets lost.
We cry too much, my master.

Hottentot Venus

Saartjie Baartman, 1789–1815

You were carried in a cage
into the theatres of Montmartre,
naked but for red paint on your face,
your mouth like a faded moon.
Your short legs paced the stage,
your large buttocks quavered
like yellow blossom on acacia trees.
You twisted your rubber tongue and clicked
repeatedly on orders from your owner,
or warbled like a bulbul.

In the secrecy of your nights did you sob?
Sister, when you died young,
the Musée de l'Homme engaged
an anatomist to amputate your buttocks
and your elongated labia,
bottle them to be displayed
beside your skeleton.
For a century and a half
the curious stood in line
to view the profile of your nothingness.

Now, the Griquas, your people,
gather you and fly you home;
your severed flesh in jars,
your ribs and grim bones held together
tenderly by metal hooks and eyelets,
in alignment.

Basket of Tears

Flashback to Sharpeville

Only cowards run away!
My uncle's insult
keeps remembering itself.
I lower my conscience
onto the palm of my hand

and leave,
watch from afar
the slow melt,
the dry birth of a nation.

Sharpeville,
a packet of sighs,
a basket of tears;
my uncle,
silica in South Africa's soil.

At the Hector Pieterson Memorial

Soweto, 2003

We walk round scores of marble bricks
strewn on a carpet of gravel   with
names of high school kids   now dead
Pieterson   Ndlovu   Makhubo....

Inside the Museum   descend the stairs
on treads of polished stone the size
of graves   In the galleries
are pictures   audios   videos:

girls in navy tunics and white shirts   boys in blazers
in the '76 Uprising   They cry   *No more*
lessons in Afrikaans   Teach in English
A photo of black and white

armed police   One blown up
haunting mural   Nzima's
masterpiece:
a tall young man in overalls runs

toward the camera   his mouth
a twisted girder   his color faded
He holds the body of Hector Pieterson
across his outstretched arms   like an offering

A stricken sister hurries alongside   eyes almost shut
Her right palm open   upright   thrusting
forward as if to stanch
the hideous tide

O My Native Land

Life was tied behind your back,
your lungs so choked by greed
you barely breathed,
I thought you died.
How glad I was to leave
the Nazi bent of Boers,
Black despair verge on rage,
play no role in the unfolding.
Then I watched you one day
proudly walk with angels
from the prison gates.

Now there are vendors
on the sidewalks; mats, beads,
hides of zebra fill the space between
traffic and the empty stores.
Merchants move to the suburbs
and to marble malls,
crowds in their thousands
aimless on the city streets.
A black man leans against a fence
breathless, skin tight on his bones.
His illness—no one will say its name.

PART THREE

Bound Close on the Naked Vine

Preface

I realize as I grow older how little certainty there is in life, how much is usurped by chance. And there are so many more questions than answers—how, for example, to reconcile oneself to the cruel beauty of nature and the inexhaustible energy of men to make war.

Maze

I veer into a cul-de-sac,
    back out to see into the life of things,

brood like organ music,
    like a requiem. I think

I know too many answers—
        end up eating crow.

     I sidestep
        the hillside of the heart,
          I've no purchase
            on that slope.

At the mirror I'm epiphany.
    Just one sperm unspooled
        my mother's egg swept up in the coup.

I could have been
        a hundred million others.

Schadenfreude

It comes unbidden,
unwelcome
as a foundling at the door
regardless of compassion—

hidden like treason,
like guilt for striving
always to have more.

It's the fault line in my vanity,
the flicker in my heart
that flares for but a moment
like insanity—when
some other person's ox
is torn apart.

Smoking

The tamping down
    the pipe's rosewood bowl
      the match and flame
        the sequence of the clouds

the suck-and-whistle
    siphon through the stem

the settling and the sinking
    the chair's embrace.

The book's indifference
    rude intrusions
bugles   bones
    another war
      another obelisk—

    O for the toehold
        at home.

The Moral Certainty of Dawn

The world keeps crashing—
   pyramids of corpses, orphans
      carved like sticks and loveless—
         with less and less to lose.

At my core I am coiled
   like the armature
      in a magnetic field,
         but the rivets
           in my heart give way—

God does not seem to care
   about my grief,

how I live uncertainly, perplexed,
   without a soul
      to cradlewrap my body in the next.

At Brewster

In memory of Henry Altman, MD

Sand flats unscarred
unspooling rafts of grass.
Miles adorned by nothing.

A canoe deserted at high-water mark
harnessed like a pony
to the seaweed-bearded cinder block.

Left and right
gulls stand steady
and face the clotted gusts of wind.

As for the tide
at the time it arrives
the beauty will claim it.

Sanctuary for Injured Birds

A pelican jerks its withered wing
            savaged by a fishing line,

        sutured-and-stapled, unbalanced.

Tall on its mended limb
        the great blue heron stands
                firm against the past,

barely sees the cages—
        cormorants, ibises, grackles
            with egg-yolk yellow eyes.

The sky, inaccessible,
            hangs there
                    like a backdrop.

Nature

I watch a sparrow pinned
on top of a telephone pole,
in the steel grapple
of a hawk who plucks
down with the skill of its beak,
to strip the calyx off one tiny breast.

Feathers fall like snow,

a remnant of the dying flails
its pinions.
The skin, the entrails unravel
like yarn. Below,
the carcass drags a wing
through last year's leaves.

Gold Vermilion

The moon's wheel rides
the rapture of the sky.

Rapt in the stalemate
of the pale succession

night is born
from a day not done,

consumed, unsung.

New Grandchild from China

For the birth mother

You loved her
when you bled her into being,
deposited your bond
in a pink wool blanket,
her cord still wet.

She has drawn
the new world in (miraculous)
through her ears,
her deep brown eyes!

How she lifts her chest for us,
to utter syllables in English—
you and she
        no longer null and void!

Love Still Rises to the Shoreline of the Lips

When the land climbed out of the sea
the hills kneeled to the stars,
and a nurseryman made a rose tree.
He cut a bud stick from a hybrid,
slid it through a cleft
in the bark of a bramble. Bound them
close on the naked vine.

About the Author

Freddy Frankel was born in 1924 and educated in the Transvaal (now Gauteng), South Africa. He migrated to the United States in 1962. His work has appeared in several publications including *Cape Codder, Concho River Review, Ibbetson Street, Moment, Passager, Senior Times, The Concho River Review, The Iconoclast, The Larcom Review, The Oak,* and three anthologies. His chapbook, *Hottentot Venus: Poems of Apartheid,* was published in 2003 by Pudding House Publications. He won the New England Writers Robert Penn Warren First Award in 2003. *In a Stone's Hollow* includes, among others, poems on apartheid and poems on World War II, in which he served as a corporal in the South African Medical Corps. A retired physician, he lives in Boston, Massachusetts.

About Sam Nzima

At 6:30 A.M. on June 16, 1976, Sam Nzima, photojournalist for *The World* newspaper, arrived at Naledi High School in Soweto to cover a student march. The students were protesting the government's new ruling that all subjects in the "black" schools were to be taught, not in English, but in Afrikaans. The police arrived and warned the crowd to disperse within three minutes or they would begin shooting. A shot was heard, and then shouts—"Skiet! Skiet!"("Shoot! Shoot!")—and he dived for cover. Moments later he recovered his wits and returned to capture the event on film.

The students ran in all directions, angry and confused. Sam saw a boy fall to the ground and a young man pick him up and run to where Sam was standing—the boy's sister was running alongside, crying. Sam clicked repeatedly as the group ran toward the press car that drove them to the clinic where Hector Pieterson was pronounced dead. Five hundred and seventy-five people died that day.

Sam knew his pictures were good, but dangerous. He removed the film from the camera and hid it in his sock. The film he replaced it with was confiscated. The hidden picture made world news. Sam gained fame and misfortune on that day. His career as a photographer ended when he had to flee from the Security Police and go into hiding. He was hunted down and placed under house arrest. It took him twenty-two years to get the copyright to one of the most famous photographs in South African history.

Sam Nzima plans to build a museum and gallery at his house near the Kruger National Park and Sabi Sands Game Reserves. He currently runs a photography school in Bushbuckridge.

(The above is a summary of a report in the *Kruger2Canyon News* 2004).

The author is deeply grateful to Sam Nzima and his agent, Heidi Smith, for permission to use the photograph in this book.

About the Publisher

Bedbug Press was founded in 1995 by Tony Gorsline, who has had a lifelong love of books and writing. Under the imprints Cloudbank Books and Fairweather Books, Bedbug Press has published twelve books of poetry, a creative nonfiction memoir, and a series of children's coloring books.

In 2003, the press established The Northwest Poetry Series with the publication of *My Problem with the Truth* by Chris Anderson. Since then three more books by Northwest poets have been added to the series: *Insects of South Corvallis* by Charles Goodrich, *Out of Town* by Lex Runciman, and *A Bride of Narrow Escape* by Paulann Petersen.

Also in 2003, the press began an annual poetry contest, The Rhea & Seymour Gorsline Poetry Competition. The contest offers a cash prize and publication of the winning manuscript. *Textbook Illustrations of the Human Body* by George Estreich (Corvallis, OR) was the winner of the 2003 contest. *Solar Prominence* by Kevin Craft (Seattle, WA) was the 2004 winner, and *Gathering Sound* by Susan Davis (Chapel Hill, NC) and *Friday and the Year That Followed* by Juan J. Morales (Pueblo, CO) were cowinners of the 2005 prize.

Bedbug Press authors have received a number of honors: Barbara Koons (*Night Highway*), first finalist for the 2006 Best Books of Indiana Awards; David Hassler (*Red Kimono, Yellow Barn*), 2006 Ohio Poet of the Year; Paulann Petersen(*A Bride of Narrow Escape*), recipient of the Stewart H. Holbrook Literary Legacy Award and a finalist for the 2006 Oregon Literary Arts Oregon Book Awards for Poetry; and Dorinda Clifton (*Woman in the Water: A Memoir of Growing Up in Hollywoodland*), featured at the 2006 Memphis Film Festival and recipient of a fellowship to the MacDowell Colony.

It is our hope that all our books express a commitment to quality in writing and publishing. Please visit www.bedbugpress.com for more information about the press.